COLORING THROUGH HISTORY

VOLUME 1

WORLD HISTORY

By Sarah Obloy

Revolutions

- → French
- → Scientific
- → Enlightenment
- → Industrial
- → conservatives/ liberals

SCIENTIFIC Revolution

ROBERT BOYLE

Galileo Galelei

Copernicus
Heliocentric Theory

SCIENTIFIC METHOD
① Hypothesis
② Testing
③ Theory

by Teacher FRANCIS BACON

Vesalius Harvey

Tycho Brahe

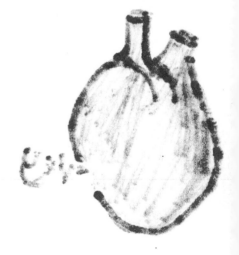

Enlightenment

PHILOSOPHE

Salons Paris

deism

checks and balances

Copernicus

Galileo

SCIENTIFIC REVOLUTION

newspapers

social contract

litteracy

NATURAL LAW

critical thinking

Encyclopedia

Hobbes

Locke

Montesquieu

Rousseau

Voltaire

THE 1800's

⇒ Industrial Revolution
⇒ Progressive Era
⇒ Imperialism
⇒ Nationalism
⇒ Unification

20TH Century

→ 3 Dictators
→ Communism
→ World War I
→ World War II
→ Cold War
→ Civil Rights Movement

WORLD WARS

→ Causes of WWI
→ Causes of WWII
→ Trench Warfare
→ WWII Battles
→ Treaty of Versailles
→ Post-War Changes

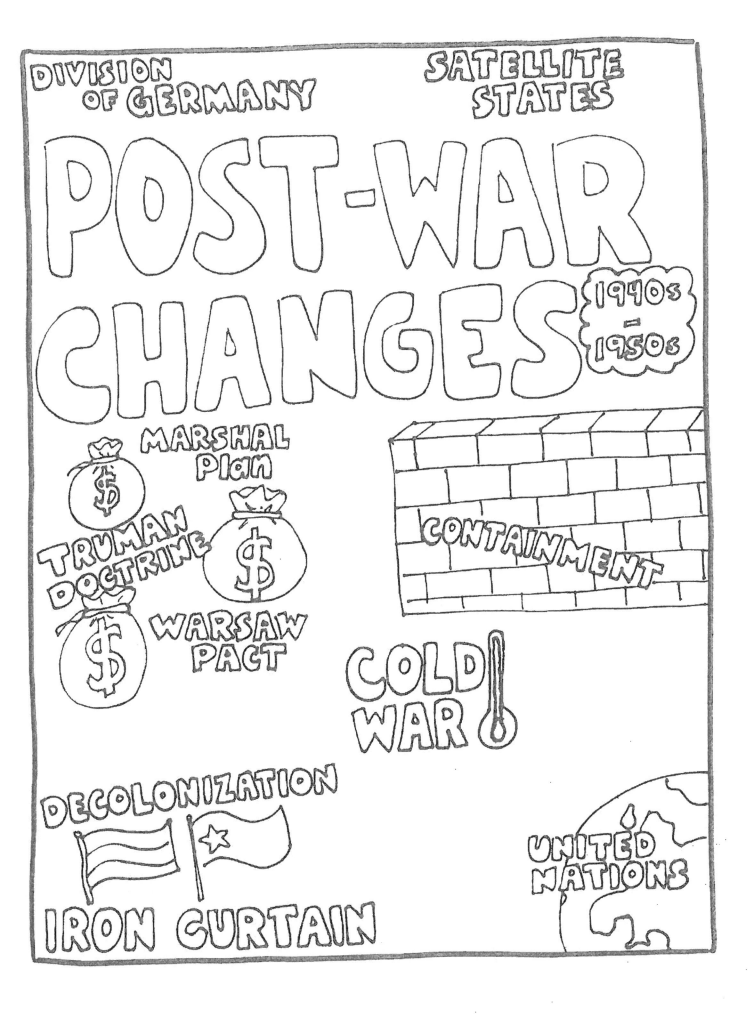

Wahnsee Conference   THE   anti-semitism

HOLOCAUST

pogroms   scapegoat

discrimination

Ghetto

Final Solution

Concentration camp

Nuremburg Laws

1935-1938

Death Camps

Victim
Bystander
Collaborator
Perpetrator
Resistor

Aryan

Einsatzgruppen

SS/SA

genocide

Kristalnacht

COLD WAR

→ Cold war
→ Korean War
→ Vietnam War
→ Space Race
→ Arms Race
→ Guerrilla Warfare

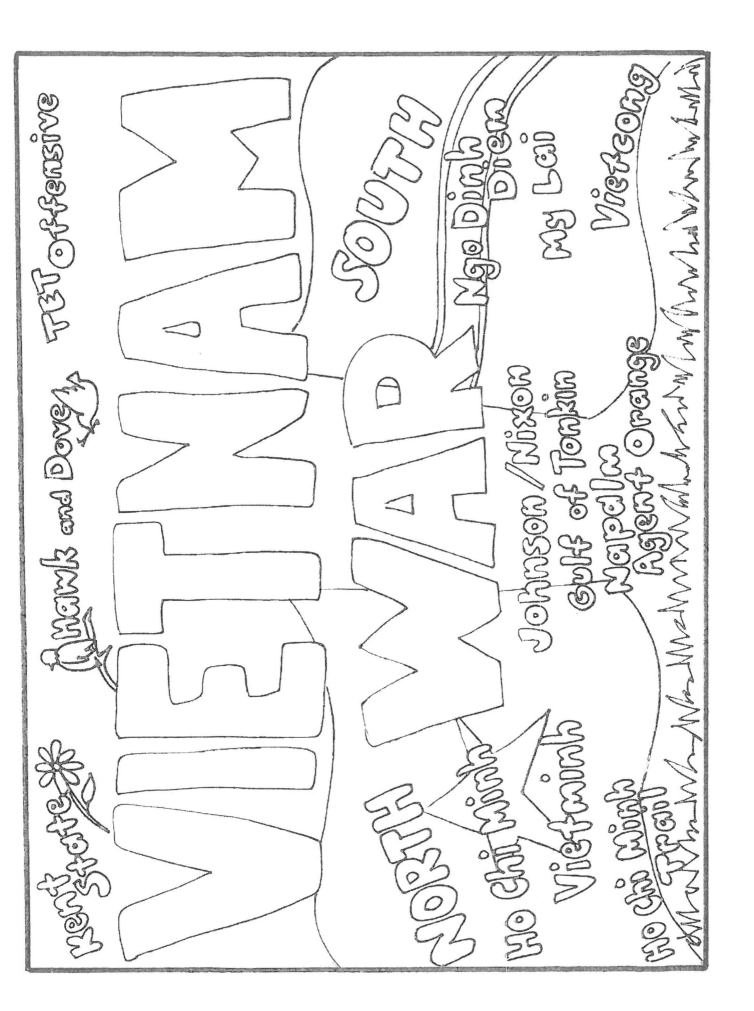

Made in the USA
San Bernardino, CA
18 November 2019